CONTENTS

WHEN DIGNITY LEFT

About 4am on 15th July
Dignity left the building
With no wave or goodbye
Dignity shut the door behind

The hours that followed
Were ones of despair and pain
Goodbye dignity
I don't think I'll see you again

With no time to be shy
No time to cover up
Within minutes I was roaring
My whole body was fucked

Never had I known pain like it
I didn't think it would be that bad
How completely wrong I was
I felt increasingly mad

I thought my life might end
Broken and distraught
But I couldn't allow my strength to leave
My, how I fought

Now you are here
I find it hard to describe
I feel elated and so lucky
So my happy tears I've cried

DAVE

I roared like a lion in your face
You didn't flinch an inch
You told me to keep still
I told you to fuck off
You didn't flinch an inch

I roared like a lion in your face
You didn't flinch an inch
You told me you'd do the epidural
You skilfully timed it in between contractions
You didn't flinch an inch

I roared like a lion in your face
Then the drugs kicked in
I looked at you and felt bad for what I'd said
You knew what I was thinking
You smiled
You didn't flinch an inch

SLEEP <small>#1</small>

I've got to sleep when you sleep
It's as easy as that
Close my eyes in an instant
And be transported out of my flat

I've got to sleep when you sleep
Such simple words to say
At least two or three people
Tell me that everyday

I've got to sleep when you sleep
Oh the panic in those words
Echoes into my head
And I cannot be heard

WATCHING YOU

Watching you lying there next to me
Twiddling your hands like you're waiting for me
I call you Windmill Arms
And ask you to count to three
Just to give me a little more time
Before the next feed

D-MER

There's a name for what you've got
D-MER it's called
The midwife borrows my phone
Look, it's there in bold

Often diagnosed as PND
That sends a whisper
Through my family

Is she depressed?
Does she seem sad?
Does she like being a mum?
I thought she'd be glad

It's D-MER, that's what it is
Not PND
Oh what a shame she's lost her sparkle
She used to be so bubbly

It was only brief
It lasted a week
Before and during feeds
I would sit there and weep

My hormones were changing
And I was still in shock
It soon balanced out
Thanks to a herbalist I got

So D-MER it's called
Not PND
I'm lucky my smile returned so quickly

I DON'T NEED ANYTHING

I don't need anything
I would say regularly
She'll live outside and run nappy free
We've got the birds, the sky, the giant lime tree

I don't need anything
I would say regularly

She'll have enough to look at
And she can play with me
I don't need anything
Oh how wrong I could be
About not needing anything
Apart from the giant lime tree

SLEEP #2

When do they sleep for longer
I hear myself say
To friends and family
At least twice a day
She will, just be patient
This is the trickiest bit
Hang on in there, you can do it
All they do is sleep, feed and shit

Oh it sounds so simple
Why am I complaining
Maybe it's because no sleep is like torture
My mind stretched and straining
Oh just hang on in there, you'll be fine
All you need is just more time

Torture is what it feels like
Tick tick tick
I want to fast forward
I want time to go quick

You'll regret saying that
Just be patient
Enjoy the moment
It won't last forever

You've said that before
I think in my head
And once again
I am reminded of bed

LITTLE MOLE

You're like a little mole
Your eyes tightly shut
Snuffling and sniffing
Burrowing through a sleepy hole

WHO DECIDES

I always wanted to be ambidextrous
Now is my chance
Eat with my left hand
Drink with my left hand
Wonder what you will be
Who decides
You or me?
I try to give things to you in the middle of both your
hands but it's quite hard to know where the middle
is.
We'll have to wait and see

ENJOY THE MOMENT

Just enjoy the moment
People say
I hear this
Almost everyday
It won't last forever
I do know that
Soon she'll be painting her nails
And moving out of the flat
It's all very well
I think in my head
But when I've had forty minutes sleep
All I can think about is bed
And I do enjoy the moment
Just not every one
There are so many in a day
But I do enjoy some

BREAST PADS

They hang up as if a reminder
Of the milk they suck up
Before washing they are heavy

A size for the day
A size for the night
Disposable or washable
Which is right?

Label side out
Inside your bra
In the dark it's hard to tell
I've never felt so unglamorous
So primal
I'm a milk machine
I hate that expression
I feel far from clean

I must smell of milk
All the time
Oh you look so natural
People tell me
Well I'm a milk machine
Amazing really, what milk does
I'm keeping you alive and breathing
With my new job as a milk machine

LOOK

I've been in this position
For an hour and a half
You smell so sweet and innocent
But I'm longing for a bath

My glass of water lies empty
Alongside cushions and nipple cream
Not yet made it to the table
Where it used to stand full and clean

I can see the tap and the kitchen
So easy and within reach
I never thought it would take so long
To refill my glass and eat a peach

I can feel your heart beating
You lift your head and rise
To check I'm still who I was
You look up with half closed eyes

And I look back
At the unreachable water
And wait

TEN MINUTE BURSTS

Everything seems to happen
In ten minute bursts
I can put you in the rocking chair
Have a shower and wash my hair
Sometimes I can make breakfast
Occasionally eat it too
And then the time is up
And it's back to me and you

SLEEP #3

You're asleep in my arms
After a long drinking session
I could put you in the moses basket
But I fear you'll just wake

Also a bit of me loves it
When you fall asleep on me
Actually I tell a lie
I love it completely

I can feel you breathing
As your growing belly moves
In and out it rises
With your fingers, feet and toes

You make little noises
Sound like a creaking door
Sometimes you sound like a cat
And then asleep once more

TRANSITION

There's a certain skill involved
In putting you in your bed
One minute you're fast asleep
The next you turn your head

Your eyes open suddenly
I feel caught in an act
You look at me like I'm tricking you
But you were asleep, that's a fact

The timing must be exact
The way I hold you, just so
If I tremble or falter
You wake and you know

I have to keep you horizontal
And move at quite a pace
So you don't feel the difference
Between stillness and moving through space

Sometimes it works a treat
Your eyes stay tightly shut
Other times I have to start again
And breastfeed through my cut

HOODIE

I used to wear a hoodie
Or at least carry it around
But since you've come along
I've been living in hot land

My body like a hot water bottle
I've worn sleeveless tops for weeks
My hoodie lies upon the rail
Discarded, free of milky leaks

I wonder when I'll wear you next
If I'll pick you up this winter
Or if the memories of wearing you
Will stay only in my pictures

Oh how I long for a hug
I realise that's why I miss you
Never did I think I'd miss clothing
Although it's replacement is untrue

SLEEP #4

Will you sleep tonight
I ask you in my head
I download white noise
Which promises you'll stay in bed

Well it lasted three hours
That's an achievement
Will I have to do exactly the same
Tonight
And tomorrow
Can't change a thing
What did I do again
What was the routine?

I can't forget it
That would be catastrophic
But my mind plays tricks on me
I think I've done something the same
Then I forget
Was that today
Or yesterday
Does it really matter
Oh stick the white noise on
And make the kitchen clatter

LAUGHTER

You laughed today
My heart missed a beat
I couldn't quite believe it
Fleeting but what a treat

A few days later
You smiled
This time your eyes joined in
Your dimple in your left cheek showed
Oh what a treat

THANK YOU PJ HARVEY

I put the radio on
Fingers crossed not heavy metal
On came PJ Harvey
With one hand I boil the kettle

She's a goodun
I tell you as you look
Towards the radio
Where PJ came out unmistook

We swayed together
You curled up in my arms
Drifting in and out of sleep
In minutes you were charmed

Thank you PJ Harvey
For lulling her to sleep
Please take this as a compliment
You nearly made me weep

SUPERDOT

You stretch, you grin
Clench your fists and shoot
Your hands above your head
Like a rocket being launched into space
You kick your legs out
Your chunky thighs stretch
You thump your feet
Your body welcoming the day

SUPERDRUG

Never did I think about
The height of the shelves
And what was on them
Until you were in a sling and we needed nappies
Size 1 nappies, who would have thought
They'd be on the lowest shelf of all.
I hadn't yet mastered the skill of bending down with
A sling without breaking you in half
You let out a cry
Oh dear, I'm sorry
I tried again
Never have I been very good at yoga
I clutch onto each shelf
We go past size 3, size 4, size 4+, nearly there
Waaaaaa
Oh no, sorry, we try again
This time just a quick bend and dip
You squeak but we get there
I feel like those grabbing machines on the pier
Only different

SLEEP #5

I see your hands and feet waving
You're asleep in your moses basket
Asleep in there for the first time
I can choose what I do
For a while I can be mine

I pace around, my mind is blank
I could hoover, cut my nails
Clean the kitchen sink
Instead I brush my teeth
Make some food
Look out the window
Then I realise I miss you
'use the time wisely'
I hear in my head
Wise words of wisdom
That I instantly forget

SHEPHERDS HUT

We're in the shepherds hut
We survived the first night
I see you having your first stretch
I see you through first light

I wait a while watching you
Wondering when you'll stir
Enough to want me to pick you up
As I know it's what you'd prefer

SLINGS

I've tried four slings
They never look right
Straps too loose or
Seat too tight
I stare at other people
Who seem to have them just right
One of your legs is always higher up
Or I feel breathless with the strap done up too tight
Have other people struggled
Before they've gone out
Sworn and sweated for twenty minutes
Twiddling straps about
It doesn't seem so
They just throw them on
And Kapow like an expert
It's immaculately done
No ruffles or ruckles
Just incredibly smooth
While I walk with you in a heap
We keep on the move

SILENT MOVIE

Like a silent movie
I watch you in your sleep
I'm keeping you alive
I am your one and only
That's what people say
What overwhelming responsibility
Which engulfs me each day
I'm giving you everything you need to survive
Without me I'm told you wouldn't be alive

EWAN

I see you in the light
Lit up by Ewan's heart
Your eyes open and close
Like an English rose
Your hands go up to your face
Then slowly back down
They touch the edge of the cot
You wake and turn around
I don't know if you can see me
As I peer behind my pillow
I take this moment in
And have a little giggle

DO THIS, DON'T DO THAT

Don't give them a bottle until after six weeks old
Give them a bottle as early as you can
Three weeks is fine
Don't given them a bottle until six months old
Remember breast is best even if your nipples are
Sore
Even if your nipples are cracked
Even if one nipple appears to be inverted
Even if you cry when she latches
Even if it hurts so much when she latches
Even if you feel sick with pain when she latches
Don't give them a bottle yet
Try a bit longer
Why don't you try until your nipple bleeds
Try until your nipple feels like it might fall off
Or be pulled off
Or ripped off
Or torn in half
Or get sucked off
But don't try a bottle yet
Oh actually why not try a bottle yet
But she might get confused
She might not feed
She might go hungry
She might get ill
Oh breast is best
Breastfeed until they're six months old
What? That's ages away
But did I say you can try a bottle?
Oh, actually no don't do that
She might get confused

Did I say she might get confused?
Or I might get confused?
Is that my baby? Have I just had a baby?
Oh I've got a baby
And she's alive
And she's a baby
Where am I? Who am I?
Did I mention confused?
No, you'll be fine
I might just have a nervous breakdown
I might just feel anxious all the time for the first few
Weeks
I might have enough adrenaline to pump a whole
Football team
I might just feel sad for no reason
I might cry for no reason
I might sweat enough for a whole football team
Oh hang on, isn't there quite a big reason?
You've had a baby
Do you think she's depressed?
Do you think she has postnatal depression?
Surely not. She used to be so bubbly
So much fun
So silly
So silly
So silly
I thought this is what she wanted
She hasn't smiled much
Or laughed
She's like a moody teenager
Oh wait; she's just had a baby
Maybe she's in shock! They are in shock.
They. Them. Together.
Do you think she'll be alright?

Cause she'll be alright
She's just been cut open to have her baby
She's just been ripped apart to have her baby
She's just been sawn in half
She's just had her muscles torn apart
Ripped apart
Cut in half
She's just had her tummy opened
Her tummy opened
Shall I say that again?
Her tummy opened
My tummy was open
She's just got her tummy muscles sawn through
Those muscles which used to be so tight
Those muscles which she worked so hard to get
Tight, to be strong
But remember, she's just had a baby
I was a strong gal
Used to be
Used to be
Used to run marathons, triathlons
Run in the rain
The dark
The hail
The sunshine
And swim, swim so much
Until I was forty weeks pregnant
Now look at her
Now look at me
Now look at what used to be me
But remember, I've just had a baby
I used to Zumba around the kitchen
Around the bedroom
Around the flat
Around the town

Around the co-op
One day you'll be able to do that again
One day I'll be able to do that again
I will do that again
All of those things
But for now I can't
Now I have you
My baby
I've just had a baby
I can barely walk
Stand
Sit
Lie flat on the ground
On my bed
In my bed
Sleep horizontal
Lie on my side
Wipe my own arse
Well I can do that one. Luckily. I'm lucky really.
Remember that
One day I'll do all the things I used to
One day. Maybe in December
Or January or March or July
One day I will
Do you think she loves her?
Do you think she wants her?
Of course she does
You can tell
I can tell
She's just in shock
They both are
They. Them. Together.
Just remember that
Just remember she's

Just had a baby
She's just done the hardest thing she's ever done
Of course she'll be alright
They will. Together.
Sweat
Did I mention sweat?
You might get so hot when you breastfeed that you
Could be in a sauna
You might have a hot flush for no reason
No reason?
Well there is one reason; I've just had a baby
A baby
A what?
A baby
Of course I love her, she's amazing
Oh isn't she gorgeous?
She's so very good you know
She's so funny
Don't you think so
Don't you think so?
Inside I think this all the time and
Am captivated
Amazed
In wonderment at my little girl
Maybe I don't show it enough
But please believe me
I truly am
But maybe I've just been cut open
Did I mention that?
Oh, and she's just had a baby
The more they sleep in the day
The more they sleep at night
Never wake a sleeping baby
Don't let them sleep past 5pm, they'll wake lots at
Night

Panic
Don't let them sleep more than two hours in one go
Panic
Or is it three?
They'll wake lots at night
Panic
They think it's nighttime
Panic
The worst thing to do is tiptoe around when they're
Asleep
Make as much noise as you can said the
Hairdresser
Said a lot of people
They need to get used to it
If they're tired they will sleep
Through anything
So I'll just put her in the middle of a noisy room
Brightly lit room
Unfamiliar room and she will sleep
Like a magic trick, just like that?
Said Tommy Cooper
Any room
Different rooms
Big rooms
Small rooms
Loud rooms
Long rooms
Small rooms
Tiny rooms
Where have you just been for
Nine whole and a bit months?
Inside a warm, dark bubble which was cosy, safe
And had sounds of
Gurgles

Bubbles
Your voice, my voice, our voices
Soothing words
Rhythm
But what, can I sleep anywhere now?
In the middle of a room?
Let's try...
She can't sleep
Train them like a dog
Don't be a slave to them
Let me spend ages
Hours
Minutes
Seconds
Soothing, calming, rocking, swaying and finally
...you're asleep.
But wait!
After all that energy, energy, on no sleep
I'll now make lots of noise just so you get used to it
And wake you up on purpose
What? Why would I do that
When I might just be able to sit for ten minutes
Five minutes
One minute
Thirty minutes
Oh no, better bang a saucepan
Just to be on the safe side
Then you'll get used to it
Oh hang on, another book, another person says
Babies need quiet
Need dark
Need comfort
Need soothing music
Need to feel how they did when they were in your
Womb

Oh hang on, another book, another person says
Don't let babies need props to help them get to
Sleep
Don't let them need you to rock them
Or soothe them
Or sing to them
Or hold them
Or be a human being and show human loving
Nature to help them sleep
You will make a rod for your own back
A rod? Ow, how painful
Or funny if you have a mind like mine and you think
Of Rodney from only fools and horses
A mind? Do I still have one? Or do I have several
Minds, several personalities from all these
Opinions, other people's minds,
Voices
Personalities
Authors of books who I don't even know
Let your child cry themselves to sleep
What?
Why on earth would I do that?
It just takes time to get her to sleep
For her to unwind
For her mind to settle after the sensory overload it's
Just been exposed to
The new people
The new sites
Sounds, smells, textures
Her new world
And that's not unreasonable
Or is it?
But then remember to make lots of noise
So they get used to it

And then all that time will be wasted
And that energy
What energy?
That energy that you had has now
Gone
But remember don't make a rod for your own back
Ow. Rodney. Where's Del Boy?
What? Ow
I'm a single mum, it's the hardest thing ever
Even if it was my choice
How old is she? Three weeks, six weeks, eight
Weeks, ten weeks
Oh, still so little
So small
So tiny
But remember make lots of noise
Just don't stress about it
Just don't stress about it
Just don't stress about it
Please tell me how to not stress
All I want is a hug
A big hug
But I give all the hugs now
Remember to look after yourself
Look after yourself
Look after yourself
Please tell me how
Have a hot bath
When?
Have a cup of tea
When?
Lie on the floor and do some breathing
When?
Watch a box set
When?

Go for a massage
When?
When they're six months old
And not before
Do baby led weaning
But don't give them anything too
Hard or too
Short or too
Fat or too
Thin
They might choke
They might die. It's happened
I heard about a baby who...
Anyway don't give them purée
They need to feel texture of the food
Baby led weaning helps them with
Fine
And gross motor skills
Being independent, learning the gag reflex
But you might just have several heart attacks along
The way
Because remember they might choke
But they need to learn to gag
From an early age
Be prepared for them not to like things
Be prepared for them to not eat anything for ages if
You do baby led weaning
But that's OK. They'll just be
Hungry
Frustrated
Wanting to eat but not being able to swallow
But remember nothing too
Hard or too
Soft or too
Long or too

Short
Oh, did I mention the more they sleep in the day,
the more they'll sleep at night
What? How?
Her cheeks are red. Her face is red
Is she teething?
Her fingers are in her mouth
Is she teething?
She's got a jumper on. Maybe she's hot
She's inside. Maybe she's hot
I've got the heating on. Maybe she's hot
Or maybe she's teething
Oh but she might not be
Maybe she's just hot
When do they teethe?
Three months to ten months
Or maybe earlier or maybe later
Or it might be somewhere in between
Or maybe she's just feeling her tongue because it's
New to her
Because she can
Because she's a baby
Sterilise everything
You don't want her to get ill
Sterilise everything
Even though you don't sterilise your
Nipples or toys or hands or clothes or other
People's hands
You don't ask other people to plunge
Their hands into boiling water for ten minutes or
Put your nipples in a saucepan for ten minutes or
Put her favourite toy in a pan
Of boiling water for ten minutes
But you must sterilise the bottle
Every day, every time you give it to her

But only after six weeks or was it three or
Six months or one day
Confused? No, course not. Or am I?
And she's only seven months old

BOTTLE

When she starts taking a bottle
Sleep will be better
Be longer
Be deeper
For both of you
I try giving her a bottle
It worked, but there's a catch
Nobody told me that
My boobs will be agony
Overflowing
Engorged
Painful like at the beginning
Oh, and because of that I won't sleep
I can't lie on my side, or my back or my front
Without pain
Don't worry they will realise they won't need to
Produce as much milk soon
Soon? When is soon?
In an hour
A day
Minute
Week a couple of weeks
Month/s
It won't last long, the pain
How long?
They still hurt a week later
What? They still hurt?
They shouldn't do. People tell me
Oh but they do, they do
They really do

FAIRY GODMOTHER

I didn't think they existed
But I found one that does
She's my mum

I look forward to her coming over
In a few minutes the flat is transformed
The washing up done
Bins changed
And Henry the Hoover out for a spin
That's the fairy godmother I know

Granny is her other name
And you grin from ear to ear
You stamp your feet
And move up and down smiling
When you see Granny walking in here

WINTER

It's snowing outside
I used to get excited
But you're not well
I'm not well
We need to stay in to get better
But that means another day
At
Home
Can't go out
Can't go through it
Or under it
Or on a bear hunt
So it's that toy again
It's pink rabbit again
Nap time?
Not quite
Nap time?
Not quite
Not quite but so nearly, so nearly
But not quite
Oh hang on, yes you rubbed your eyes
Oh good
It's definitely naptime
But for how long?
Ten minutes
Twenty minutes
Forty minutes
I don't want to risk
Boiling the kettle
Getting something out of a rustly bag
Coughing too loudly
Flushing the chain

But make lots of noise
The voices in my head whisper
I try to shut them out
Trusting my intuition is what it's all about
As time fades so too will these worries
But not yet
We're in the thick of it
In the centre of it
And in the centre is you
You are the centre of everything
My little bundle
My little bear with
Little ears and wispy hair
Nap times are precious
And an achievement each time
I'm lucky I'm fairly stable
If I wasn't, I wouldn't be able
To cope with not knowing
From one second to the next
An onslaught of emotions I find
So complex
So it's another Thursday, Sunday
Tuesday, Friday
Every day is a day we haven't had
Before yet it feels like we have.
You eat now
You need breakfast
Lunch, dinner
We're together, we go out,
Come back, chat, play, dance and laugh
Get ready for bed by having a bath
And another night begins
I'm lucky to have you
You're my one in a million
My one and only

My fork and spoon
My knife and fork
My shoes and socks
But it's fun to share you
To see other people
Friends
Family
To get us through those days that
Drag
'Don't you just love being a mum'
My friend said to me
Of course I do but actually
I find it pretty
Hard
Work
On my own
But I don't like to moan
So I don't say that bit
I keep it to myself
And think I can do this
So many people do this
On
Their
Own
And don't moan
You're lucky
I'm lucky
We're lucky to have each other
And that's all that matters
Don't wish time away
Enjoy every minute
That's what they say
You'll regret it if you don't
Part of me has never felt more present
I have to be here

With you
If not
You know
But also when 7pm comes round
I'm ready to lie on the ground
And be still…
It's 6.30
6.35
6.37
Only two minutes later
Nearly 7 not quite
Nearly
Phew… Made it
You're in bed
I close the door
Lie on the sitting room floor
Put Channel Four news on
Wonder what colour
Jon Snow's socks are today
And his tie
Don't relax too much, there's
Dinner to make
Bottles to shake
Surfaces to wipe
Washing up to do
Tidying up to do
To do
To do
So many things.
Then the biggest of all…
Sleep
In a heap
Or not.
Or stay awake
Trying

Desperately
Hard
To
Sleep
And I can hear you
Snoring your way through the seconds
Hours, minutes of sleep which
Lie ahead
And rapidly go
Or seem to last
Fore v e r
Another hour
Another hour
Tick tock tick tock
Sleep when she sleeps
You must otherwise
You'll be so tired
So tired
So tired
But then you wake
After ten minutes of me being asleep
And I try not to cry
Or be cross
As I feel the sleep leave my body
And force myself to get up
Attend to your needs
Your wants
Your pleads
But in the morning
When it's finally morning
When morning arrives
When nighttime is over
When all those hours have gone
When twelve hours have gone
When thousands of seconds have gone

And daytime is here once more
I see you and sing to you
And you greet me with the
Biggest
Smile
I can see the back of your throat
You beam
I beam
We beam
And all the nighttime wakings can be
Forgotten
Once more as I hold my head which
Feels
Sore.
This won't last forever
I hear people say
No but it's going to go on
For more that one day
It's like a merry go round
Like the carousel on the pier
Round and round the garden
Like a teddy bear
Getting dizzy
On repeat
Getting dizzy
On repeat
But you're so worth it
My little bear
And each day you're growing up
Up and up
And we will have a garden soon
For you to go round and round
The garden
You can dress up like a teddy bear
I will too, I don't care

We live in a flat now
Up two flights of stairs
I've bought a house
You'll have your own room
I'll have my own room
We'll have our own rooms
I might miss your snuffles
Your whispers
Your gurgles
But we'll live in a house
And still see the sea
And you'll learn to crawl
Walk
Dance
Run
In our little house with me
We'll have a square of grass
That's all we need
To get out of the house quickly
And do as we please
Our little house waits for us
At the top of the hill
Many adventures to come
With you, my baby
And me, your mum

WIPE

I wipe your face
The table
My face
The floor
Your bum
My bum
The kitchen surfaces
The highchair
The bath
Your hands
My hands
Your nose
My nose
Then repeat
Then repeat
Then repeat

DANCE

We're like a dance
You and I
We come together then we say goodbye
You fly about in your walker
While I wash up
You lick the curtains and smile
Then drink from your cup

You're learning independence
A little more each day
You like your space at the moment
Exploring and learning to play

You're good at telling me
When you've had enough
You'll make little sounds
Sneeze, hiccup and puff

ALL CHANGE

Everything changes at six weeks
People keep telling me that
But when I get to six weeks
I find out it's not a fact

Everything changes at eight weeks
People keep telling me that
But when I get to eight weeks
I find out it's not a fact

Everything changes at three months
People keep telling me that
But when I get to three months
I find out it's not a fact

Everything changes at six months
People keep telling me that
But when I get to six months
I find out it's not a fact

Everything changes at nine months
Yes I think I finally agree
Although not everything
And I still struggle to finish a cup of tea

GRANDPA

You see Grandpa, a smile beams over your face
You stretch out your arms and wait for his embrace
He's a strong Grandpa who holds you tight
You feel safe in his arms and within his sight
When he visits us and we open the door
Your eyes light up and are with him once more
He plays the guitar and you watch his hands
The music transports you to foreign lands
You like his watch and you squeak with delight
You try to eat it but it doesn't taste right
You wave your little arms when he leaves to go
And peer out behind the curtain of the window
Goodbye Grandpa and we wave together
We are lucky to have Grandpa with us forever

SUCH A HAPPY BABY

Ooh she's such a happy baby
Such a joy to be around
She never cries or is upset
Must be easy really, not making a sound
That's when I want to scream
She's not always like this!
You see the best of her!
Try getting up all night and then having the day
Without a break and a cold cup of tea to stir
The mornings go on for weeks sometimes
Before the morning nap
Making breakfast, having a shower
Eating breakfast standing up
Then there's clearing up
Tidying up
And getting ready for the day
Making sure lunch is healthy
Making time to play
Of course she's worth it
You are worth it, you know that
But sometimes I feel exhausted
And you want my attention and won't have a nap
So there's no time to tidy up and wash up and get
Things ready for the next few hours
Because I'm the only one here and I don't have
Special powers
And then someone else tells me:
Oh she's such a happy baby
And I want to scream
Not always! That's a fact!

STRESS

It rises like a whale
Deep down in the sea
One
Two
Three
And it appears
Burrowed in the depths of me
Maybe it lives in my bones
And has been there all along
Or maybe it's new to me
Since the day you came
Along
It can happen in a second, drowning my senses
It takes over like an elephant
Stampeding over hedges
It comes closer and then swallows me up
I can't see
Hear
Smell
Taste
Or Touch.
The stress takes over my body
The feeling is immense
Falling down a dark hole
My body feels tense
I rub my eyebrows
My mind races
I want to feel calm again, but don't know how
There is always a reason when it happens
And where we can't escape
When you're hungry
Thirsty

Tired
All in one go
In need of a quiet place
Sometimes we're on our way home
Halfway up the hill
Hang on we're nearly there
I say
You struggle to be still
Or sometimes we're with people
And I see you about to tip
I gather up our things, hoping you don't flip
I know it's not that bad
And things will be ok
It's just in that moment of panic
We need to escape with no delay
Sometimes you just need your bed
To be at home and familiar
Or just a bit of space is needed
Which people find hard to give you
Because you're irresistible

FUCK, SHIT, BOLLOCKS

I think your first word might be shit
Or fuck or bollocks
You've started eating
Sometimes you sound like you're choking
Fucking Fuck is what I say
Or shit heads

We met some friends today
You stuffed in a mini rice cracker
It disappeared from sight
You could hardly close your mouth
I couldn't fish it out
You looked like a hamster
And then you swallowed

You went red, you gagged
I started sweating
Your eyes watered
And you kept gagging
It's OK said my friend
Fucking Fuck is what I said
You looked at me
Then you coughed
Then it came back up

Then as if nothing happened
The day carried on
Fuck shit bollocks is what I say
With a variety of words added each day

TWO HOURS IN TOWN

I skipped down the road
Because I could
I walked between scaffold poles
Because I could
I walked beside a beer barrel delivery van that was
Parked on the pavement
Because I could
I walked on the curb
Because I could
I sat with a friend in a café
We played three in a row
I know her!
I know her!
I know her!
We chatted and drank tea
She asked what my news was
I just bought a new pair of sunglasses
I bought them for a fiver
On Kensington Gardens
Because I could
I enjoyed my peppermint tea without spilling it
Without it going cold
Without saying Hot, it's Hot
Because I could
We sat in the window seats
I crossed my legs
Because I could
I walked to the counter to order my drink
I swayed as if pushing you
I took time to chat to the waitress
Because I could

I nipped into the library on the way home to go for
A wee
I went in the regular toilets
Because I could
And then it hit me
Like a big lump in my throat
I missed you
I walked at quite a pace
Then I trotted
Then I went back to walking because it was too hot
I walked up Islingword Street in record time
I broke into a sweat
I walked quickly round the corner
Up Queen's Park Road
I couldn't wait to see you
Because I could
Aren't I lucky I thought
To see a beaming smile when I walked in the door
Because I could
And I hugged you
Because I could

WISE OWL

You are high up in my head
Like a peak on a mountain top
Keeping an eye on the land below
Without the need for words

Like a wise owl you keep a watchful glance around
Not missing a thing even though you may not hear
Every sound
When I see you and the youngest together
I feel proud
There is a connection
Without the need for words

I know that she knows that you know each other
We look up to you and always will
You are the one we follow
Without the need for words

The silence that ebbs and flows when we are
Together
And when we go
Speaks more than the need for words
And we love you and always will

FRIENDS

I couldn't have done this without you
You all know who you are
Those who have been friends forever
And new ones from near and far
There are friends that are parents already
And I text you random worries like:

How do you sleep when they sleep, will swimming
help blast the crap out of her nose, she's sitting up
in bed waving and has been for 2 hours and won't
go to sleep, when can I face her forwards in the car
she's facing backwards and wondering where I am,
oh no she's fallen asleep at 5pm and hasn't had
any dinner or milk would you wake her, does a
sheepskin keep them cool in Summer…

Then friends who don't have babies
Who are equally important to us
Friends who we don't see very often
But there's still a strong connection
I'd like to see you more
To share chats and affection

We'd be in a heap without you all
It can be tricky being a mum
But I know you'll all be there
In the days, months and years to come

BACK TO WORK

Our time is nearly up
We won't ever get that again
The time we spend together
Through sun, wind and rain
I feel sad to see it going
As each day fades away
We have created special memories
The two of us
Enjoying time to play
The first few weeks were stressful
I think we both felt shocked
But we got through it
And got to know each other
Now we're solid as a rock
I will never forget the feelings
Of those early months
I feel proud to spend time with you
Even through the bumps
The endless nights of breastfeeding
Of holding you to sleep
Then putting you in your cot
Hoping you won't peep
These are disappearing
And you like your own bed
You smile when we climb the stairs
In our new house
You grin and lift your head
We have a bedtime ritual
Which really helps a lot
Bath, massage, song and milk
And safely in your cot
You now have a bottle

Before you go to sleep
It took a while to adjust
And still depends how much you eat
We sleep in separate rooms, only a wall apart
Sometimes it feels like miles away
Especially in the dark
My ears are tuned into you
Each time you make a squeak
Woken up suddenly
I get up and have a peak
You like to move around now
I see you hiding behind the curtains
You have found your own game
Grinning to yourself
You do it again
You pull things off chairs
And lick anything you find
Your tongue is your detector
And speaks directly to your mind
There are cats in the neighbourhood
They come up to the door
Your face lights up when they appear
You couldn't believe what you saw
You say Taa and wiggle
And smile with delight
Throw your arms and legs about
And say it more and more
If I could pay the cats to entertain you
They would be very rich indeed
Especially between the hours of 4 and 5pm
When you are waiting for your feed
And so our time is nearly up
We won't ever get that again
But we will always be together
Through sun, wind and rain

Printed in Great Britain
by Amazon